COMBAT MISSIONS:

Flying the B-24 Liberator

Bomber Out of Manduria, Italy,

450th Bomb Group,

720th Squadron,

WWII

A Memoir

Burl D. Harmon

Foreword by

William "Bill" E. Smith, Ph.D.

BookBaby Publishers

Pennsauken Township, New Jersey

2022

The Library of Congress title of work: Combat Missions: Flying the B-24 Liberator Out of Manduria, Italy, 450th Bomb Group, 720th Squadron WWII.

Registration Number: TXu 2-320-057, Issued July 26, 2021.

Cover design by Lily Ray and H. Hayes

Author Photo: Flight training graduation photo

Top Aerial Photo: "The Sandman a B-24 Liberator, piloted by Robert Sternfels", Wikimedia, 2004, https://commons.wikimedia.org/wiki/File:The_Sandman_ a_B-24_Liberator,_piloted_by_Robert_Sternfels.jpg

Bottom Aerial Photo: "Formation of 450th Bomb Group B-24s Flying through Flak." Wikipedia, 2004, en.wikipedia.org/wiki/720th_Bombardment_Squadron

ISBN 978-1-66785-696-4 (paperback)

ISBN 978-1-66785-697-1 (eBook)

Manufactured in the United States of America

To Nancy, my beloved Daughter, and Dan, my son
the eternal optimist, who left us way too soon.

Acknowledgments

For nearly eight decades, I have carried memories about my military experiences in WWII and sometimes shared my stories with friends and family. When Western Washington University Retirement Association opened a second writers' group, I jumped at the opportunity to write brief episodes of my tour of duty. My fellow writers listened to my stories with deep interest, which further spurred my enthusiasm to keep at it. My wife, Nanette, active in her writers' group, and a multiply published author, urged me to consider putting the stories in a memoir. My first response to this idea prompted a quizzical remark: "Who'd want to read another war story?"

She countered: "Your daughter, for one, and me, and all your closest friends. Furthermore, it's a hallmark of history."

I realized that not many WWII veterans were still alive when I researched the 450th Bomb Group archives for information on my former crew members. My preliminary findings yielded no results, and I can only surmise that none of my crew members lived.

Significant among my supporters have been seasoned and published writers Catherine Shornick and Bill Smith. John Logan, an army veteran, bolstered my flagging writing energy. A special mention to Jim Ciborski, the son of WWII airman, Jim Ciborski, Sr. with whom I flew several combat missions. As historian of the 450th Bomb Group, Jim's knowledge and understanding of the era surpassed any other source.

Without the boost from my wife, Nanette, and daughter, Nancy, this book would never have seen the light of day. As my faithful editors, Nanette and Lynda Jensen helped transform my sometimes-rambling prose into a finished product. Lily Ray offered great assistance locating old photos and military archives. Only I, however, can take responsibility for the accuracy and readability of my story.

Foreword

In his memoir, *Combat Missions: Flying the B-24 Liberator Bomber Out of Manduria, Italy, 450th Bomb Group, 720th Squadron, WWII.*, Burl Harmon, 78 years later at the age of 97, describes the impact of WWII on him, a 19-year-old from Boone, Iowa. After being drafted in 1943, unable even to drive a car, he found himself the flight engineer of a B-24 Liberator Bomber, responsible for the mechanical safety of an "Ugly Duckling" on 38 combat missions from March to October 1944. Thirteen of those bombing missions to Ploesti, Romania were so dangerous that the U.S. Army Air Corps counted each of them as two missions, increasing the crew's tally from 38 to 51.

In one year, Harmon attended eight 6-8 week training schools, slowly transforming from a small-town boy to an integral team member, experiencing for the first time camaraderie, teamwork, brotherhood, and "the spirit of unanimity." His training expanded his world, taking him to Detroit, Atlantic City, Long Island, Puerto Rico, Cuba, and Texas before combat, and later stationed in Manduria, Italy. His descriptions of a flight engineer's duties throughout a flight reveal how much he learned in one year.

He meets an assortment of people on each of his travels, from one egocentric crew-endangering pilot to his incredible crew members who show him camaraderie and team spirit. He recalls Spike Jones's performance at the

Stage Door Canteen, escaping a brothel in Havana, the Trepaldi family who ironed uniforms in Manduria, and kind strangers who welcomed him home.

He vividly describes the severity of problems caused by the wounding of his navigator and the danger of his B-24 separating from formation to return home alone. He praises the P-51 escorts flown by the intrepid 332nd Black Squadron, Tuskegee Airmen, who accompanied his squadron. Their "Red-Tailed" presence raised crew morale and led him to avow, "Without a doubt, I am alive today because of their heroic efforts."

After his combat tour, he visits Boston on his way home and musters out at Mountain Home Army Air Base in Idaho, where he taught new officers and crews the functions of battle stations. A young lieutenant praised his teaching and opened the mental door for him to attend college and become an English teacher.

Returning home, he confronts civilian life, learns of his parents' impending divorce, the loss of his longed-for girlfriend, and enters a new entanglement initiated by his mother after she proudly placed one of his letters in a newspaper. Months later, he enters college and begins his new 40-year trajectory as a high school teacher and administrator.

Harmon's anecdotes and details move far beyond a simple initiation story to a story of momentous transition confronting millions of Americans. Harmon captures the resilience, responsibility, and acceptance of war and its implications. As he writes in his "Introduction," "even though the implications of WWII tested our democracy…

our task ahead is to continue to integrate those left out, the marginal among us, into the fullness of American life."

Years later, as the narrative moves to an end, Harmon reflects on ten memorable characters from his missions. He lists their acts of brotherhood and sadly reports that two died (one in combat and one in a possible PTSD-related accident), and another spent the remainder of the war in a series of Nazi prison camps after being shot down. One, whom he considered his closest brother, he sadly lost contact with and "never connected after the war."

Harmon writes a circular narrative that begins shortly after his 19th birthday and describes the induction center, training, furloughs, bases, combat missions, mustering out, and memorable people who impacted his life. He closes his circle half a century later when he and Nanette, his wife, both retired educators, sign on to offer American English classes in Ostuni, Italy, for Global Volunteers. While there, they visit Manduria—the site of Harmon's former airbase and see the homage villagers paid to American forces. Unable to connect to the Trepaldi family, a heavy sadness follows him home.

Burl Harmon's *Combat Missions* captures a young boy's growth to adulthood under dramatic character-shaping circumstances. He gifts us all, especially his family, friends, and former students, with an engaging memoir that depicts an insecure time through a thankful senior veteran's eyes.

William "Bill" E. Smith, Ph.D.
Professor Emeritus, Western Washington University

Vice President, Board of Directors, Growing Veterans
(2014-2020)

Praise for Combat Missions

As a veteran and a son of a veteran from World War II, this book accurately depicts typical combat missions. Harmon came to the fight after heavy losses, which made the triumph of the war more exciting. A thoroughly entertaining read.
—John Logan, C.P.A.

Burl has done a lovely job capturing his youth, innocence, growth, wonder, responsibilities, challenges, fear, respect, and personal journey during this altering and life-changing time for him (and the nation and world). It's a journey on many levels, beautifully expressed.
—Catherine M. Shornick, a member of Burl's Writing Group, Western Washington University Retirement Association.

A marvelously well written, engaging, and compelling book ...Such great stories! And so well told that I felt I could see the events unfolding and feel the feelings of those in the stories!
—Alana-Christina Dittrich, MSW

Contents

Introduction

Why give an account of my combat experiences 78 years after I served in the military? I want to demonstrate how carefully Uncle Sam prepared us to fight, recognizing this could be both an extensive war and an enormous loss of life. In the period of a year, I had eight training sessions, extending an average of six to eight weeks, learning my job as a flight engineer for the B-24 Liberator bomber.

I did not incline toward developing manual or mechanical skills. I could neither drive a car nor even ride a bicycle. Training to become familiar with a war machine presented a frightening challenge. Our American recruits were mainly boys, subjected to parental authority. In the wink of an eye, military rule subjected us to a momentous transition. Unlike our former life, we had to shape up: take orders promptly! The military brooked no arguments, no back talk, no lewd comments, and especially no standing out in the crowd. For 31 months, I would think as a team; act as a team; survive or die as a team in a single spirit of unanimity.

Another reason for this writing entails the importance of historical memory. Keeping in mind the unmitigated horrors of battle, this war, the most important American military engagement of the 20th century, initiated some of the most far-reaching social changes in the US: the increased significance of high-level technology; the integration of women, and less successfully, Blacks, into the military; the deep involvement of citizens in the war effort; and the opening of higher education to millions of veterans.

War is not a game. This reality needs reinforcement. Today, when gaming has become a national pastime, and players spend millions of dollars yearly on this entertainment, our collective sensitivity to real war has been forgotten. Characters in war games can rise repeatedly, but in actual conflict, the sacrifice of victims is permanent. War has never been a final solution. As World War II demonstrates, the aftermath of this conflict has been significant social and political upheavals that have generated more human strife, including the Stalinist takeover of East Germany and Eastern Europe by Communist regimes.

I have lived through extraordinary events. Yet, my life in the Army Air Corps was full of ordinary moments of friendships, travel, new experiences, deep learning, and the ability to take on profound responsibility for myself and others.

Given the high-level risk of flying imposed in those dangerous days, those of us who made it back can feel intensely fortunate that we survived. In addition, my gratitude goes out to all the people, those I knew and those I did not, who supported and prayed for me and for our cause. World War II tested our faith in American democracy like no other occurrence, and through enormous efforts, we emerged victoriously. Our task ahead is to continue to integrate those left out, the marginal among us, into the fullness of American life.

Chapter 1.   Day of Infamy

A sea of students crowded into the high school auditorium and stared at the serious face of our principal, Larry Evans, who strode onto the stage and asked for quiet. He adjusted the microphone, cleared his throat and spoke. "Today we have a message from the President of the United States." I heard President Roosevelt's voice booming out over the loudspeaker.

"Yesterday, December 7, 1941, a date which will live in infamy...I ask that Congress declare that since the unprovoked and dastardly attack by Japan on Sunday, December 7th, 1941, a state of war has existed between the United States and the Japanese Empire." This news had an ominous ring in my ears.

I was eighteen years old. For the next year and a half, I enrolled in eleven hours of junior college courses and worked at the local Rexall drugstore. Having received my draft notice, I realized that my days as a civilian were about to be over. I quit my job at the drug store, and went to visit my relatives in south central Missouri. I thoroughly enjoyed the attention of my aunts and uncles and particularly the good country food that was typical of every meal. I also visited my grandmother, who was still living, who always saw me as her first and favorite grandson. Time dragged on, still I wasn't drafted, and I finally returned to my hometown of Boone, Iowa.

Quite a few of my classmates had enlisted in the Army Air Corps but others, like me, were waiting for Uncle Sam to call us into other branches of military service. On the morning of March 16th, 1943, my dad drove me to the bus bound for Fort Des Moines, Iowa. Both my dad and I sat in stony silence because we had never talked about my being in the army. That morning my mother had bid me goodbye at home and said that she would pray for me. While we waited to board the bus, my father suddenly burst into tears, and cried out.

"It's not fair, you're too young. They should have taken me."

My father deeply loved me, feelings he had never expressed before. I stumbled out of the car blinded by my tears and boarded the bus. World War II started for me on that chilly morning.

Fort Des Moines Induction Center was a merry-go-round of activity. Upon arriving there, it became crystal clear that we were to do as we were told. Excited, scared, and hungry to the point of nausea, we were herded into the supply room. There we were measured for uniforms, fitted with shoes, and told to package up our civilian clothes for mailing home.

My recollection of army food is hazy but we ate out of hunger. After dressing in our new attire (scratchy wool uniforms), we filed into a medical center and were given shots in both arms. As I recall, it seemed as though every time we walked through a door a guy had another needle to press into our sore arms.

Living quarters called barracks were our next assignment—a place to stash our barrack bags, the army's equivalent of a suitcase. The evening meal (chow) took place in a room called the mess hall, an accurate operative term: army food is a mess. As an effort to cushion the culture shock of a new lifestyle, the army put on a show to entertain the new inductees. A stand-up comedian told one joke and I recall what he said,

"You know what a bachelor is? He's a guy with no children to speak of."

His feeble effort at humor did little to enliven my spirit or relieve the developing soreness of my arms. I wasn't the only one. None of us had any inclination to clap.

Chapter 2.   Manhattan Transfer

For several days we traveled on a troop train from Fort Des Moines, Iowa to the East Coast, our final destination. The training field was at the boardwalk in Atlantic City, New Jersey of all places, where the Army taught close-order drills and military courtesy. They issued M1 Garand rifles and instructed us in the manual of arms. I never expected to ever see Atlantic City in my life. Here I was in the middle of it!

Our barracks, located in five-star hotels stripped to the wall, had government issue beds and other military equipment, creating an austere environment. I remember a sergeant speaking to us about the care of our uniform.

"Go to a tailor and have it fitted right because you are going to wear this for the duration of the war, and this can go on for a long time. I urge you to take pride in your uniform."

I was deeply impressed, not only by his words, but also his commitment to the uniform. I determined then to do the right thing: my uniform would always be impeccable. To this day I like to be fitted correctly with my trousers, a knife-blade crease without cuffs.

On our first aviation mechanic school training, we were stationed at LaGuardia Air Force Field, Long Island.

Having never been to a city larger than Des Moines, Iowa, I felt disoriented by being jostled about by teaming throngs of commuters, some of whom were pushy and angry. After floundering from block to block, I found myself at 42nd and Broadway. If you can be lonely in a crowd, I certainly was. Lonely beyond comprehension in the mad rush of people, bound for somewhere, maybe nowhere. I wondered what to do. I was so lost and confused. I never really liked New York at some level. I was always by myself, because I thought I was the only guy who wanted to explore the Big Apple.

The much-hyped Stage Door Canteen urged service members to drop in and meet movie stars, radio personalities, and others in the performing arts who would talk, drink coffee, and dance with you. In truth, none of this ever happened. I walked into an empty room. Nobody was there, much less movie stars. Finding a Pepsi-Cola service center and getting free tickets to the movies (less 28 cents city tax) lessened my disappointment.

Best part: I had a chance to see "Casablanca," starring Humphrey Bogart and Ingrid Bergman. Just as I was leaving the theatre, the curtain opened on stage, and orchestra members filed in with instruments in hand. It was none other than Spike Jones and his City Slickers wearing red uniforms with coonskin hats. What a laugh! The audience went wild, hooting and screaming. This orchestra was best known for creating parodies of other songs. An hour later, sides aching from hilarious slapstick comedy, I made my way out of the theatre, relishing and re-living the show by a favorite comedian, who was my idea of a great entertainer.

Lodging on a weekend pass from the military post was always a challenge. I learned quickly that some facilities were free and welcomed service members, and some did not. The Salvation Army furnished a bed and shower free of charge, but the American Red Cross did not. Negligible but still charging, the Red Cross made us poor service members pay thirty-five cents for a single accommodation. I avoided that outfit like the plague.

Similar to a peacetime tourist, I took an elevator to the top of the Empire State Building and the Chrysler Building, and then walked over to Grand Central Station. I was in total awe at the grandeur of the buildings and the magnificent view of the city from 100 floors up. A guide located at the Empire State Building said to us,

"If you drop a penny from the top of the Empire State Building, and it strikes the top of a car, it will cut a hole in it, just like a bullet." I found later that this was a myth for gullible out-of-town tourists like myself.

My all-time favorite Manhattan tourist attraction was the New York City Public Library. It seemed incredible that the library had an entire floor dedicated to western novels by Zane Grey, my favorite author. For the first time since I came to this city, I felt at home. Little by little I learned my way around on the subway to places of interest in New York, feeling very cocky about how familiar I was becoming with the city. Later I would brag to my fellow soldiers from the East Coast about my newly discovered abilities to get around.

"In a couple of months I'll know more about your town than you do, and you'll stay as dumb as you are now."

But New York City never had my heart. One often hears that the Big Apple is a fabulous place to visit, and I agree. But with my small-town upbringing, I would never want to live there.

Chapter 3.   Casey Jones School

The training seemed endless. After we finished our first round of gunnery training that involved firing at a target from the cockpit of an airplane in Brownsville, Texas, our next destination was Newark, New Jersey to train at the famous Casey Jones School of Aeronautics. We had two training shifts, calisthenics in the morning and classes in the afternoon and evening. There was no time for dinner with this schedule, so the evening meal occurred at 11 p.m., after which we retired until the next day. The only exception was on Friday night until midnight Sunday, when we were given much-needed time off.

This zany schedule seemed idiotic. After working all day and night, we grumbled to one another about the late supper. But the army had no choice. Facilities were so limited it was the best accommodation they could muster.

All the Catholic boys would skip the evening meal on Saturday, race to showers, dress in class A uniforms, and prance out to midnight mass. Having completed their church duty, they proceeded to paint the town red until two or three in the morning. Upon returning to the barracks, where we were all fast asleep, they would turn on all the lights and wake us up. The barracks erupted in anger.

Everyone was pissed that these drunks had disrupted our sleep.

On one of my most memorable weekend passes on Long Island, I had a unique experience. As I was walking toward the subway, a chauffeur-driven DeSoto car pulled up, and a distinguished looking lady rolled down the window, and said,

"Soldier, where are you going?"

"I'm headed for the subway at Mineola Station," I told her.

"We're going that way, but we have one stop, and we'd love to give you a ride."

"Yes, Ma'am. Thanks."

For the next 20-30 minutes, the kind lady treated me to a sightseeing tour of elegant homes in that well-appointed community. During the ride, the lady opened her purse and handed me her calling card. Mrs. Arthur Crawford Glass III, was inviting me for an evening with her family.

"We'd love to have you come next Wednesday evening for dinner."

To say that I was elevated to the stars, is an understatement. I had never met anyone like this genteel person. This experience taught me there are warm, friendly people wherever you go.

To my utter dismay, that much-longed-for dinner never happened. Our squadron shipped out Tuesday to Detroit. Tongue-tied at 19-years old, I couldn't tell Mrs. Glass that the Army had different plans for me. To this day, her memory lingers with the soft notes of regret.

After completing our six-week training at Casey Jones School, our group transferred to Ford Motor in Michigan where machinists assembled the B-24 bombers. Before leaving Michigan, I bought a folk guitar, hoping to relax with my buddies throughout the intense training. This guitar traveled with me for almost all of my tour, entertaining many homesick fellows. This second round of gunnery training took another six weeks. Here, the military schooled us in the complex systems of our bomber.

Upon finishing this training, the Air Corps moved our class to yet another military gunnery school in Laredo, Texas. Considering it was a balmy October, they issued unseasonal winter uniforms. By the time we arrived in still summery Texas, we were uncomfortably dressed in bulky, wool uniforms. I recall the grunts and groans of our formation every morning, as we forced ourselves into the unyielding, hot clothing.

As we headed for days of the boring troop train passage to Texas—and more gunnery training—the sergeant in charge, who just happened to come from Texas, promised us.

"Boys, you'll love Texas so well, you'll want to jump off and stay."

The rejoinder from one G.I.

"Sarge, you were right. If I ever saw a jumping-off place, it's Texas. How much sage brush, cactus, and flat lands can a guy stand?"

Since I've always been a foodie, I usually remember meals, all sorts of meals. But my memory of Army food fades. It seems, from today's perspective, overly plain and ordinary. The coffee I vividly recall because the military carefully corrected for contamination by using excessive amounts of chlorine bleach. In fact, that's all we could taste was the bleach: the worst coffee of my life!

We went to the post exchange (PX) for relief from army grub, where they sold the tastiest egg salad sandwiches. As a teetotaler, I dutifully drank Coca-Cola®—too much of it—to get rid of the chlorine and bitter coffee taste. To this day I cannot tolerate the taste of that popular drink.

I could hardly wait to leave this land of pink grapefruit, long-horned cattle, and lyin' Texans. I grew weary of hearing the tired joke by non-Texans.

"Sure, you'll love Texas, and be sure to see the outlying areas!"

"What outlying areas?"

"Nobody out lies the Texans."

Chapter 4. Gunnery School: I'm Ahead of The Game

Training absorbed every waking moment that first year after induction. My training stations—Detroit, Atlanta, Long Island, Puerto Rico, Cuba—every one proved formidable because each air base offered an entirely new learning experience. Brownsville, Texas, turned out to be the exception because training here focused on guns. I felt totally prepared. You could say I was ahead of the game, coming from a rural area and later, a small town, hunting with my father and my uncle to furnish wild game for food. I was supremely comfortable handling and shooting guns, but the guys from big cities or suburbs had never held a gun, let alone shot one. I thought, here is the place I can really excel. I was feeling quite smug about these gunnery exercises.

As soldiers, each of us had to fire and qualify with four weapons: a .22 rifle, the .30-06 Springfield WWI (which if you didn't hold correctly could bruise a shoulder), the Garand M-1, an army favorite, and a shotgun. When faced with an actual gunnery test situation, I suddenly found myself fearful that I couldn't make the grade. When the sergeant informed me that I had met the minimum standards to qualify as Marksman, I deemed myself fortunate just to qualify.

Next step: we piled into the bed of a pickup truck and rode to the gunnery range for trap shooting. This exercise turned out to be invariably challenging because this time I had a *moving* target, part of the strategy of tracking enemy fighter planes. It was a fairly routine exercise, and I achieved this at a moderate level of accuracy. At least I improved over the minimum grade from the earlier test.

I learned early never to point a gun at a person. As the sergeant put it more graphically: "Don't point that barrel at anyone you don't intend to shoot."

The sergeant's warning pointed to a larger picture, a focus on safety. Air training involved multiple risks: handling guns, being airborne, lacking experience, and normal human error. I learned to be cautious at all times, following all the safety standards and procedures. I wasn't alone. Every member of the military was confronted with unfamiliar challenges. One mistake could cost lives, equipment, and jeopardize the war effort. In my entire year of training, I never witnessed nor heard about any significant safety violations. This has to beat any civilian record!

I vividly remember the first time I was airborne. Arriving at the flight line at 7 a.m., I stopped short, awestruck by the beauty of the sunshine. Shafts of red-gold clouds resembling an artist's rendering of a latticework lit the early morning sky. Could anything go wrong with such a brilliant omen?

The sergeant interrupted my brief reverie, barking out an elaborate set of instructions to our small group of 15 men, preparing us for air-to-air-conflict. We worked in teams of four.

"This is a .30-caliber machine gun, mounted in the second cockpit of a Texan AT-6 training plane. You will each be assigned to a plane, one man to a plane, and take your seat behind the pilot. Each gunner will be issued two 100 round belts of .30-caliber ammo. Each belt of bullets is tipped in various paint color codes with each gunner receiving one color: red, blue, green, or yellow. Your job is to fire at the canvas target being towed by a moving plane about 200 yards out. The bullet hole in the tow target determines each gunner's accuracy."

More coaching: I sighed with relief. I sat quietly behind the pilot as he provided more instructions.

"Fire at the first one-third of the tow target for the best accuracy."

I followed his directive, but to my horror, I fired too far ahead and severed the tow rope. The target folded like a tired accordion and sank into the Gulf of Mexico. Mortified, I was absolutely certain I would be court-martialed, a humiliating end to my military career.

"I'm sorry, Lieutenant, that I cut the tow rope. I guess I'm the only one who didn't make the grade." What a goofball, I said to myself.

"No problem, soldier," the pilot said, "we'll just come back and do this again in the afternoon. Sorry, you'll miss your afternoon nap," he grinned.

I came back after lunch, followed the same procedure as the morning, jumped into my seat, and the pilot took off, cruising at around 2,000 to 2,500 feet. I felt relieved and grateful that the officer didn't punish me, but even more, gave me a second chance.

Just getting into the airplane the first time gave me the willies. But this time I got it right and considered myself a real champion with a pretty good score.

Chapter 5.   Hello Cuba

Our next training program was at Chatham Field, Atlantic City, Georgia. In the deep South, we had good warm conditions for ground-to-air drills. But shortly after, literally rained out, we couldn't continue the training. In its wisdom, the military flew us to sunny Cuba to complete the ground-to-air training—for only a couple of days. Just enough time to spend in Havana.

The sergeant in charge of our squadron gave us a much-needed pass until midnight to "take a look around Havana." I didn't realize that it was necessary to caution us to "always go in pairs or more."

"There are a lot of poor people here who'll stick a knife in you for a couple of US dollars. So, what do you want to do, boys?"

A chorus of guys shouted out, "Girls! We want to get laid."

"That would be the El Trocadero," they told us.

I asked the obvious question from a kid from the sticks, "What's that?"

"It's a whorehouse, stupid," was the rejoinder.

A newly married guy, Jimmy, and I were terrified. We had no interest in consorting with these "hookers." Like tens of thousands of G.I.s, Jimmy rushed to the altar before the military sent him overseas.

To keep up appearances, we piled into an open-bed truck along with the others, drove through a seedy part of town, and were duly deposited at the "El Trocadero." When we pulled up to our destination, Jimmy asked "what the hell is this place?" It was the famous El Trocadero—a whorehouse. Stuck in a dark alley in the roughest part of town, the building looked decrepit. We were greeted by the madam when we entered.

"Hello boys," said the Jamaican-born madam in an educated English accent as we entered, "you've come to the right place."

Standing in a circle around her were twenty to twenty-five scantily dressed gals, wearing only panties and a brassiere: straggly girls, with makeup smeared heavily across their faces. This first impression dampened any enthusiasm we may have had for entering the bordello in the first place. Still quivering, Jimmy and I could think of only one thing. How can we get out of this?

The cost was a whooping two dollars for only a few minutes with a girl who appeared to be little more than a teenager. The system worked this way. There were two columns of girls on each side of the room. Each guy would pay his money to the Madam, run the gauntlet, and a girl would step out and choose a guy and take him upstairs. Jimmy and I exchanged looks of terror, as weak-kneed, we started to back off from this sordid business. But not soon enough.

One of the girls pointed to me, and said "Rojo," referring to what the Army said was my sandy-red hair. My face was probably redder than my hair. I muttered to Jimmy, "How do we get out of this?" I didn't even want to contemplate having sex with this girl. She totally repulsed me with her unhealthy looks.

Jimmy and I were uninterested in these girls for different reasons. He was newly married. I had absolutely zero sexual experience, and this was hardly my idea of first love. When the girl called me "Rojo," she had made her choice, and gave me oversize goose pimples at the thought of any connection with her. I needed out. Fast!

"Let's check with the boss, Jimmy. We haven't paid yet."

We went to the Madam and told her we had to leave because we had to get back early to report. A lie, but she didn't have to know that. At first, she brushed us off, telling us to go ahead and get one of the girls. We hung back, shaking our heads. We wanted out of there, but how? Finally, we just gave up and paid the madam as if we had had one of the women. What a damn relief to walk out of there. Jimmy and I had one thought: we escaped getting the clap!

The two of us walked down one of the main streets of Havana and were impressed with the beauty of the buildings and people. I recall one couple, who wore a black and white suit and a dress to match, as they leisurely strolled down the street. As we meandered through the main streets exploring the Spanish, Colonial-themed architecture in the tourist area, I was surprised by how clean the streets were. Cuba was a city untarnished by war, but we could not fully appreciate it at this stage of our lives. We went back to the truck, two lonesome country boys, to wait until midnight to go back to base.

Chapter 6.   Going to War

In late May 1944, we ferried a squadron of twenty-eight B-24s, four formations of seven planes. We were assigned barracks and issued combat flight gear. After a few days, our training crew was reassigned, much to our dismay, so each of us would fly combat with someone we didn't know. As a flight engineer, I was the liaison between the crew chief and the pilot. One of my duties was to safety-wire each gas cap and oil cap with soft brass wire. This action prevented the slipstream from siphoning the fuel overboard. The other duty involved inserting the nose wheel pin to secure the nose wheel.

Each evening we checked the bulletin board for the next day's flight assignments. I can't remember all of them, but here are some of the flight crew with whom I flew most of my missions: pilot Jack Holler, copilot John Fredd, navigator Harry Fine, radio operator Mike Friebolin, ball-turret gunner Al Chartier, and waist gunners Jon Leahy and Melvin Dean.

On May 31st, 1944, I flew my first mission with Lt. Colonel Robert Gideon, Base Commander, with whom I flew only once. Our target, Ploesti, Romania, had deep reinforcements that often led to casualties. I only learned later that this was undoubtedly the most dangerous target in the European theatre.

My battle station was the top turret. Six battle stations mounted twin .50-caliber machine guns: nose, top turret, ball turret, two wing turrets, and the tail turret. Compared to the B-17, the B-24 Liberator wasn't considered a glamorous plane—like the swan to the ugly duckling—but it did the job. We carried a larger payload, and we flew farther than the B-17, the Flying Fortress, featured in many Hollywood films.

Our flight gear included an oxygen mask, a flight suit, a .45-caliber pistol, a parachute harness, and a parachute pack. It was always tricky to wedge into my seat with the bulky, sheepskin flight suit.

Combat missions took six to seven hours. Our purpose was to destroy Hitler's oil supply and supply depots. We also had diversionary targets, such as Munich, to draw off the Axis Air Force planes' defense of Berlin.

I had arrived in May 1944, and D-Day was just a month away. Activities at the air base were somewhat routine. We were supposed to fly combat missions an average of one flight every three days. Exceptions occurred frequently. I had five sessions flying three or four days non-stop. In one stretch of time, September 6th through October 7th, 1944, I flew nine missions in a row, prior to ending my tour of duty.

We were mainly on our own during off days: doing laundry, writing letters home, and hanging out in the local town. This easy-going routine could be interrupted with close-order drill, if the base commander decided to keep us all in shape with endless marching.

Once a week we received a few items to boost our morale: two cokes, one beer, two packs of chewing gum, two candy bars, five packs of cigarettes, and two cigars. Harry Fine, at 25, an old guy to us, loved cigars. Harry said, "bring me a handful of envelopes and I'll censor your letters home—you know, what not to write." In return for his generosity, each of us gave him our cigars. A tradition among GIs is to have all their buddies sign a dollar bill and attach a bill from each country they have been stationed in throughout their tenure. Harry's sense of humor: crossing out Henry Morgenthau, the Secretary of the Treasury, and signing Harold E. Fine, and above his signature, U.S. Army Air Corps.

Chapter 7.   My First Combat Mission

Here I am; it's my first combat mission. I wonder what Mom is doing? Probably sitting by the bedroom window reading the Bible and worrying about me. I'm located at the Army Air Force airbase at the arch of the boot in Manduria, Italy, our airbase, making it convenient to launch combat missions to the Balkans. With the Adriatic Sea virtually at our doorstep, our home base made it possible to reach our Eastern European targets in three to four hours.

At 7:00 a.m., I wolfed down my breakfast, grabbed my flight bag, located my assigned plane, and dumped my gear on the deck, right behind the pilot. I took a deep breath as I clambered through the top turret and onto the wing, 15 feet off the ground. From this precarious position, I quickly wired each gas and oil cap. That done, I climbed back down to the flight deck, closed the hatch, and checked my gear: parachute pack, harness, oxygen mask. I was task-ready but feeling apprehensive.

I waited for Lt. Schwab, our co-pilot, to line up our plane for takeoff. Then, I crawled down to the nose wheel section and, once airborne, pulled the nose wheel pin and laid it in a safe place. Airborne and at 200 feet above the ground, I could look down through the nose wheel, and see how dangerous this job really was. If I lost my footing, I could fall out of the nose wheel and be a statistic. This dire event did not happen. Success! I was off to a good but shaky start for my first mission.

As I hastily crawled back up, out of the nose wheel and into the top turret, I heard John, the copilot (when airborne, we used first names) announce over the intercom, "Today is the big one—Ploesti, Romania!" My belly wouldn't stop quivering. Although my flight suit was thick sheepskin wool, I was still cold. On the bomb run, the temperature was 15° Fahrenheit. Strange to say, I found it difficult to stay awake because the oxygen made me sleepy. Over and over, I struggled against nausea as my stomach lurched into my throat.

When we crossed the Adriatic Sea into the Balkans, Glenn called me, "can you do the fuel transfer now?"

"Roger," I said, and set the valves to pump gasoline from the wing tanks to the main tanks. I felt relief, and experienced terrific pride in carrying out this essential duty.

About four hours out, we approached the target, and straight ahead, I saw puffs of smoke—flak! The smoke was rising over 20,000 feet just ahead of us. The plane lurched wildly as Victor opened the bomb bay doors and dropped ten 500-pound bombs that fell four miles below. I could almost hear the ground shake, although you couldn't hear anything through the noise of a nearby bomb explosion.

Suddenly, one of the waist gunners yelled on the intercom, "number four plane at 5 o'clock got hit, and I counted three chutes that got out." I wondered how many others made it. I was scared shitless, feeling my plane could be next. "Am I gonna die today?" I asked myself. Our squadron made a broad sweep away from the bomb run, and I felt the knot in the pit of my stomach ease a little. I still felt the shock of that plane going down and feared for those who wouldn't get back to safety.

Flying back to our base, I kept thinking that I would have to do this again and again. Actually, as I found out later, I would fly at least every three days or more often. As we approached the downward leg of the airstrip, the pilot lowered the landing gear and the nose wheel. I inserted the nose wheel pin, and we touched down. We all took a very deep breath.

Mission accomplished, I thought to myself. Who thought this farm boy could handle a bomber to keep an entire crew safe and gassed up for the entire flight? This experience was the real thing after all the training, I kept murmuring to myself. And, by God, I'm still alive. I had to relish this moment because in three days, we would be assigned to another target, and I'd have to go through that damn flak again.

Two Red Cross gals met each crew as they landed—I thought they were absolutely gorgeous—making fresh, hot donuts. I would always look forward to these interludes, the pretty girls and their welcoming donuts that greeted us on each return—such a heartfelt connection with home. The medics showed up, as well, with their medicinal reprieve.

"OK guys, get out your canteen cups. Here's a shot of whiskey."

Being an obedient son of a Baptist mother, I gave away my booze to Mike, the radio operator. I ate the donuts, though, and you can bet I can still taste them!

Chapter 8.   Ugly Duckling

I owe my life to an exceptional machine: the B-24 Liberator. By official description, the B-24 is a war plane: a four-engine bomber, designed to transport 10, 500-pound bombs. The aircraft had a crew of 10 members: four officers—pilot, copilot, navigator, and bombardier, and six sergeants—covering the battle stations. My position on what I fondly called the ugly duckling was the top turret, located at the top of the ship, behind the wings and the fuel tanks. When I was assigned this position, I knew that it could be very precarious, open to enemy fighters who flew over the squadron.

Compared to the elegant B-17, the "Flying Fortress," featured in many Hollywood movies that I mentioned previously, actually looked like it could fly with a sleek aeronautical design. Our ugly duckling, by contrast, had a flat bottom and the Davis wing, which had no glide angle, compared to the more famous B-17. Yet, the payload and airspeed of the B-24 proved significantly greater. Most notably, the B-24 had a cruising speed of 350 miles per hour and a range of 800-1000 miles, a fast plane for a bomber in that era.

I cherished my job as an aviation mechanic, just one of two recruits, to fill out the Army Air Corps quota. Once I learned that my classification was that of flight engineer, I was both amazed and terrified. For one thing, I couldn't even drive a car, and for another, I felt terrified to be responsible for the critical tasks I would have to carry out.

Most guys my age yearned to have a car of their own. My father, a body-and-fender specialist, had restored a 1939 Chevy to running order as our family car. Despite what my dad called "his best effort" to teach me the rudiments of driving a car, he was grossly disappointed when I "just couldn't get the hang of it." Why I failed, I'll perhaps never know. Maybe, Dad wasn't the most patient teacher for the job, always snorting at the slightest error.

The military seemed to assume every G.I. could drive. At one point, an officer told me to "take this jeep over to the repair depot." Shamefacedly, I had to admit, "Sir, I don't know how to drive." His reply: "You don't know how to drive? Good God, man, I thought everyone knew how to drive a car."

The B-24 saved my bacon. Okay, I couldn't drive a car, but I knew my job on this aircraft: safety wire the gas and oil caps, insert the nose wheel pin on landing, and transfer fuel during the combat mission. I also operated the twin-caliber machine guns, which for me was a remarkable achievement. I had an overweening pride in my role as the flight engineer.

As a member of the 720th Squadron, our plane was one of four called the Cottontails, a point of honor. Our aircraft had vertical stabilizers, two upright structures that kept the plane upright in flight, painted a bright white, so very easy to recognize. Of some concern, our 720th Cottontails attracted the attention of "Axis Sally," an American woman turned traitor who served as a disc jockey on the FM radio station from Germany. Her intention was destructive. Her scratchy voice over the radio accused us of machine-gunning the German pilots who had bailed out of their ME-109 or Focke-Wulf 190 aircraft. "Not true," we said and laughed at her propaganda but found her "big band" music much to our liking. "Sentimental Journey" had to be everyone's favorite!

My job as a flight engineer involved starting a two-cylinder hydraulic system (a lawn mower, putt-putt), designed to generate pressure to raise and lower the landing gear and activate the brakes once the plane touched down. On every flight, this task was always a source of anxiety for me. Will the damn putt-putt start? What can I do if it doesn't start? We couldn't land without disaster; it would mean the brakes won't work! Disaster! Fire! Explosion! We're ruined!

Sure enough, on one of my last combat missions, as we touched down and moved into the taxi strip, I heard the dreaded words called out by the pilot, "We've lost our brakes!" Our aircraft, headed for a parked plane, collided and severed a fuel line, allowing a one-inch stream of 100 octane gasoline to spill out. We moved quickly without speaking, following training procedures, scrambling off the plane to safety.

White-faced, trembling, and silent, all of us walked rapidly back to our barracks. I had not failed to turn on the engine. The hydraulic system had failed. It allowed us to lower the landing gear, but sputtered out because of a fault in the hydraulic line. Dealing with such an event underscored for me the risk of war, always threatening, always alarming, sometimes deadly.

Chapter 9.   Stationed in Italy

The Trepaldi Family.

Although Italy was not the Army's version of a tourist mecca, I found delightful diversion with an Italian family, the Trepaldis, as well as a three-day furlough to Rome.

Every evening at sundown, I could see tiny arcs of light that looked like fireflies blinking in the distance from the village of Manduria. Curious, I asked my ball turret gunner, Al Chartier, what they could be.

"Those are charcoal irons women swing to press their clothes; they're hot and dirty, but they get the job done." Al went on to say, "the heating process begins by fanning the charcoal, the women swinging them in an arc, switching hands until the embers grow red. It takes strong muscles to move these huge clunkers. Still, I've never heard of anyone who dropped their hot iron."

Al had met Luco Trepaldi and his wife, Mama, as she was called, with her brood of eight children ranging in ages from three years old to 19-years old, when he looked for someone to clean his uniforms. He offered to bring me along.

"Let's take our suntans (summer uniform) and get them washed and pressed. Mama Trepaldi does a great job."

From then on, twice a week, we traipsed to the village to turn in our soiled uniforms and pick up the clean ones. The Trepaldi family was a joyful release from the military base, always so welcoming to the two of us displaced boys. Part of the attraction, to be sure, was the two Trepaldi sisters, Lavina, 19, and Tina, 17, who sat with us while their mother finished the laundry. Once in a while, under a parent's careful gaze, we were allowed to hold hands with the girls, but nothing more.

Somehow, a chaperone was always there, Mama Trepaldi with her steaming iron or Papa Trepaldi with his water glass filled with homemade red wine. Neither parent seemed to work outside the home, a condition shared by their neighbors: all impoverished victims of war.

The girls were always dressed in sparkling, starched white dresses, impeccably ironed, of course. Our conversation may have been limited to food and the weather, but Tina loved to giggle, regardless of the topic. Lavina presented a more reserved manner, looking aslant at us. Dressing up for the conquering heroes, the girls were always the highlight of my day.

My Italian grew to three phrases: "Buongiorno," "Grazie," and "Que Cosa Dice," so I could greet the family with a bright good day, thank them for their courtesy, and ask them how they're doing.

Al and I would have gladly paid for the laundry service or simply for the privilege of holding these darling girls' hands, but the Trepaldis refused to accept money.

"What can we offer them?" I asked Al.

"Let's get one of those survival kits and give it to Mama Trepaldi. I've got an extra one she can have."

These were C-Rations, comprised of a vegetable mixture of carrots, potatoes, celery, a single can of cheese, one bar of dark chocolate, and one cigarette package, such a dribble of food for a family of 10.

In its retreat some months earlier, the German Army captured every morsel of edibles: chickens, pigs, cattle, cheese, and anything left in gardens. I was so ashamed of bringing this small token to these half-starved people. In completely removing the town's food supply, the residents had little or nothing to sustain them. Only after our arrival could the villagers return to some semblance of normality, growing gardens again.

Nick, our barracks man, an exuberant 15-year-old, used to go to the end of the chow line, and before we could scrap our plates, he carefully took our leftovers, scraping the food into a gallon bucket. This fed his family for the day. I could only imagine the stewed tomatoes and brown gravy poured over the no-longer luscious cherry pie.

When we handed Mama Trepaldi our paltry offering, far less nutritious than the leftovers Nick pulled together, she burst into tears of joy. I would have happily stolen an acre of food from the mess hall and taken it to these hungry souls, but I lacked the courage.

Chapter 10.   All About Jack

The Army Air Corps offered a welcome release from the rigid class structure of the Army or Navy. When a non-commissioned officer encountered an officer on the base in the regular Army, it was obligatory to salute. Those of us in the Air Corps rarely saluted—Okay, we gave homage to our commanding officer, the Colonel in charge. The salute is shorthand for the deference lower ranks owe higher ones. That's why Jack Holler immediately stood out as a guy who demanded deference, whether on or off the base.

Once in a great while, you found an officer who had worked himself up through the ranks to a commission, a highly esteemed achievement. Jack Holler was one of those lucky guys who made the grade of lieutenant, but rather than being viewed as a hero, he was often considered "difficult." We soon tired of Jack's outsized ego, non-stop bragging about his rank as first lieutenant, and what a "great man" he was.

He incessantly told us, "When this tour of duty is over, I'll make captain, and then try for squadron commander. I've got what it takes."

I met Jack about halfway through my tour of duty in Italy, having flown with him a couple of times. I got to know

Jack pretty well and continued to remain under impressed. Here's the braggart blowing his own horn again.

"Imagine this, guys. I waited until I was drafted and then immediately applied to be an air cadet, even before being assigned to a position. The brass knew my value and pushed me straight into the right spot."

Like every bomb group here, we had six battle stars, but like most guys, we never talked about it. That was not the case with Jack.

"Look at this! Six battle stars. Wait until the folks at home hear about this. My name will be plastered all over the local newspaper."

It wasn't only his arrogance that had me rolling my eyes, but three more features made this self-important lieutenant unlikeable to high and low ranks alike. Jack treated more subordinate ranks as lesser; he took undue liberty with situations; and he was aggressive to the point of breaking the rules.

One early bright sunny afternoon—and Italy had so many of these—Jack burst into the barracks.

"Harmon, on the double, fella. I'm pilot today. Grab a parachute and meet me at plane #252. We're doing an engine check on a plane the ground crew chiefs said needed one. You're flying today!"

Jack didn't mean combat. He was using the engine check as an excuse to fly over to Naples, where his wife was stationed as a military nurse. Of course, engine checks every 50 hours were mandatory after seven missions to guarantee an efficient operation. Engine checks are relatively short procedures, but Jack's flight from Manduria to Naples was two hours one way. And for what purpose? To bed down his wife! So, what could I do with the hours of waiting? And what about a first lieutenant taking out a $250,000 airplane for his own pleasure?

"Stay with the plane, Harmon. No time for you to get lost in Naples. I'll be back in an hour. Just sit tight."

Glumly, I sat in the plane. What the hell was I supposed to do during the hours of his escapade? Nor did I ever see Naples during his fooling around times, which well surpassed his "hour," a sure way of keeping me in line.

Jack never had anything to say on his way home on those flights that took another two hours back to the base, a total of over six hours. Jack pulled this stunt a couple of more times before another incident stopped him. Jack was never called out for this leisure time travel with me as his only hand-picked flight crew, possibly because no one except me knew about his pastime. The military's male culture taught me not to be a whistle blower. Another possibility? Jack was allowed to get away with it.

Bragging and pushing the envelope to the very edge were not Jack's only character flaws. Another incident demonstrated how Lt. Holler reflected his attitudes toward life in general and flying in particular.

Our target one early August morning in 1944 was the bridge between Italy and Switzerland, the only route the Nazi army had for retreat. We knew it was a highly strategic mission, and that meant no mistakes. After dropping 10, 500-pound bombs, we skirted swiftly away and headed for the base: mission accomplished. We were all very jumpy after that last bomb run, eager to get back and unwind.

Still, we were number six in the flight pattern, which meant we had about five or six minutes until the first five planes landed. That's when Jack blew his gasket, deciding to speed up in a devil-may-care approach!

Ignoring his place in the line-up, Jack banked sharply, tilting precariously to the left, cutting number three plane out of formation in the landing pattern. We came down hard with the plane still not stabilized, bouncing on the left landing gear, and skewing the plane to the right, coming down even harder on the right landing gear. For a minute there, it looked like doomsday for all of us. The ground crew chief said to me later, "I thought Holler was going to crack up on the landing strip, and take you guys out. Landing a plane on one gear is just plain dangerous. What the hell was he thinking?"

The Air Corps kept detailed accident reports. The following is a photo of the accident report, dated June 25th, 1944. The report lists the crew members and the specifics of the accident for which Lt. Holler was severely reprimanded.

WAR DEPARTMENT
U. S. ARMY AIR FORCES

REPORT OF AIRCRAFT ACCIDENT

ACCIDENT No. 127

44-6-25-504

(1) Place Manduria, Italy   (2) Date 25 June 1944   (3) Time 1340

Aircraft: (4) Type and model B-24H   (5) A. F. No. 41-28607   (6) Station A.P.O. 520

Organization (7) 15th (Command and Air Force)   (8) 450th Bomb Gp (9) 720th Bomb Squadron (H)

PERSONNEL

Duty		NAME (Last name first)	Rated	Serial No.	Rank	Personnel Class	Branch	Air Force or Command	Result to Personnel	Use of Parachute
(10)		(11)	(12)	(13)	(14)	(15)	(16)	(17)	(18)	(19)
P		Holler, Jack S.	P	O-812594	2nd Lt.	18	A.C.	15th	None	No
CP		Williams, Paul P.	P	O-750906	2nd Lt.	18	A.C.	15th	None	No
B		Myers, Doyle A.	B	O-708959	2nd Lt.	18	A.C.	15th	None	No
E		Barmon, Burl D.	E		M/Sgt.	38	A.C.	15th	None	No
R		Deem, Melvin A.	R		Sgt.	38	A.C.	15th	None	No
AE		Leahy, Joe F.	AE		Sgt.	38	A.C.	15th	None	No
AR		Larsen, Elmer	AR		Sgt.	38	A.C.	15th	None	No
AG		Jackson, Stanley B.	AG		Sgt.	21	A.C.	15th	None	No
AAG		Chartier, Alfred A.	AAG		Sgt.	38	A.C.	15th	None	No

PILOT CHARGED WITH ACCIDENT

(20) Holler, Jack S. (Last name) (First name) (Middle name)   (21) O-812594 (Serial number)   (22) 2nd Lt. (Rank)   (23) 18 (Personnel class)   (24) A.C. (Branch)

Assigned (25) 15th A.F. (Command and Air Force)   (26) 450th Bomb (Group)   (27) 720th Bomb Sq. (H) (Squadron)   (28) Frantic A/D (Station)

Attached for flying (29) 15th A.F. (Command and Air Force)   (30) 450 Bomb Gp. (Group)   (31) 720th Bomb Sq. (H) (Squadron)   (32) Frantic A/D (Station)

Original rating (33) Pilot (Rating)   (34) 9-25-43 (Date)   Present rating (35) Pilot (Rating)   (36) 9-25-43 (Date)   Instrument rating (37) (Date)

First Pilot Hours:
(at the time of this accident)

(38) This type	42:00	(42) Instrument time last 6 months ... None
(39) This model	42:00	(43) Instrument time last 30 days ... None
(40) Last 90 days	42:00	(44) Night time last 6 months ... None
(41) Total	42:00	(45) Night time last 30 days ... None

AIRCRAFT DAMAGE   NF

DAMAGE		(49) LIST OF DAMAGED PARTS
(46) Aircraft	See Attachment	See Attachment
(47) Engine(s)	See Attachment	
(48) Propeller(s)	See Attachment	

(50) Weather at the time of accident CAVU

(51) Was the pilot flying on instruments at the time of accident No
(52) Cleared from Frantic A/D   (53) To Frantic A/D   (54) Kind of clearance Combat

(55) Pilot's mission Secret

(56) Nature of accident Taxi accident

(57) Cause of accident Personnel error.

RESTRICTED

Fig 1. Accident Report, ack Holler, Pilot, Page 1

DESCRIPTION OF ACCIDENT

'Brief a. . v . . . id .m. Include statement of responsibility and recommendations for action to prevent repetition)

On returning from a combat mission on 25 June 1944 Lt. Holler landed his B-24H aircraft, serial number 41-28607, on the runway and applied the brakes. On the initial application the outboard brakes failed due to the line from the accumulator to the brake selector valve breaking. The inboard brakes stopped the aircraft satisfactorily and Lt. Holler taxied approximately one mile around the taxi strip before the collision.

On leaving the taxi strip Lt. Holler realizing he had no brakes, cut the engines on his airplane and allowed it to roll into a parked B-24H aircraft, serial number 42-52443.

The pilot was at fault for the following reasons:

    1. He should have stopped the aircraft at the end of the runway and permitted it to be towed to its parking place.

    2. He should not have cut the engines on his aircraft and thereby lose directional control while his aircraft was rolling towards a parked airplane.

It is the board's opinion that if the engines were running, the pilot could have controlled the direction of roll of his aircraft and thereby have avoided the accident.

Airplane 41-28637 has been turned into the Service Squadron on the base and should be serviceable in approximately 30 days. The attached work sheet from the 331st Service Squadron lists the required work to place the damaged aircraft in commission.

Signature

JOHN S. MILLS, Major, M.C.

ROBERT R. GIDEON JR. Lt. Col., A.C.

WILLIAM G. SMAITH, Lt. Col. A.C.

Date 26 June 1944

Fig 1. Accident Report, Jack Holler, Pilot, Page 2

Here's the text of Page 2 of the Accident Report for clarity.

"On returning from a combat mission on 25 June 1944 Lt. Holler landed his B-24H aircraft, serial number 41-28607, on the runway and applied the brakes. On the initial application the outboard brakes failed due to the line from the accumulator to the brake selector valve breaking. The inboard brakes stopped the aircraft satisfactorily and Lt. Holler taxied approximately one mile around the taxi strip before the collision.

On leaving the taxi strip Lt. Holler realizing he had no brakes, cut the engines on his airplane and allowed it to roll into a parked B-24H aircraft, serial number 42-52443.

The pilot was at fault for the following reasons:
1. He should have stopped the aircraft at the end of the runway and permitted it to be stored to its parking place.
2. He should not have cut the engines on his aircraft and thereby lost directional control while his aircraft was rolling towards a parked airplane.

It is the board's opinion that if the engines were running, the pilot could have controlled the direction of roll of his aircraft and thereby have avoided the accident.

Airplane 41-28607 has been turned into the Service Squadron on the base and should be serviceable in approximately 30 days. The attached work sheet from the 331st Service Squadron lists the required work to place the damaged aircraft in commission."

Jack's renegade pilot days may not have been over, but I believe he was transferred to another squadron because I don't recall seeing him again. I doubt that his dream to make captain, much less squadron commander, would ever happen after this accident.

All air combat missions are close calls, granted. I've reflected on that close call a number of times. But this was unnecessarily aggressive and needlessly risky behavior that put an entire crew and airplane in jeopardy. Jack Holler will always remind me of the self-centered guy who refuses to follow the rules and, without thinking, puts everyone else's life in danger.

Chapter 11.   Bomber Escort Cover

The other side of bombing Axis targets involves the fighter escort planes. From May to October 1944, I flew 38 combat missions, protected by pursuit planes, the P-38 twin-engine attack craft and later the P-51 fighter planes, piloted by the intrepid 332nd Black Squadron, Tuskegee Airmen.

For the first part of my Italian mission, the P-38 flew cover for our bombardment groups. As we approached the target, German aircraft constantly harassed our planes. The escort cover had limited protection though, hampered by lack of maneuverability, requiring a seven-mile circle to engage the enemy fighter planes.

About halfway through my tour of duty, the Army Air Corps deemed the P-38 fighter cover planes too slow, cumbersome, and ineffective. The situation changed dramatically once the Black Squadron daredevils began their dive-bombing and strafing missions against the German attack planes. The sleeker, more agile P-51 plane with its single-engine quickly replaced the older P-38 fighter plane.

The all-Black squadron served with distinction in World War II from May 1943 through June 1945. The fabled "Red Tail" presence in the 15th Air Force raised the morale of several bomber crews, who often requested to be escorted by these fighter pilots. Without a doubt, I am alive today because of their heroic efforts.

My admiration for the Tuskegee airmen grew from realizing that the Jim Crow laws, still extant during this period, had outlawed Black soldiers from becoming pilots. In 1941, fewer than 4,000 Black men were serving in the military, and only 12 Black men had become officers. By 1945, more than 1.2 million Black soldiers served in uniform on the home front, in Europe, and the Pacific, including thousands of Black women in the women's auxiliaries.

The National WWII Museum, located in New Orleans, honors the contributions of the Tuskegee Airmen in World War II by highlighting some of their exceptional achievements. I will be forever awed by these intrepid pilots.

"The Tuskegee Airmen flew more than 15,000 sorties between May 1943 and June 1945. Bomber crews often requested to be escorted by these 'Red Tails,' a nickname acquired from the painted tails of Tuskegee fighter planes, which were a distinctive deep red. Sixty-six Tuskegee Airmen died in combat. They had one of the lowest loss records of any escort fighter group...In all, the Tuskegee Airmen earned eight Purple Hearts, fourteen Bronze Stars, three Distinguished Unit Citations, and 96 Distinguished Flying Crosses."[1]

Despite the P-51's excellent cover, our crew had a near-death experience with a group of German Focke-

---

[1] https://www.nationalww2museum.org/sites/default/files/2017-07/tuskegee-airmen.pdf

Wulf 190s, who whizzed over our plane at speeds of up to 350 miles per hour. I paraphrase my navigator who reported that the waist gunners, who could see the action, told him about the destructive attack on the bomber just ahead of us.

"There's a bogey at 4 o'clock high, and I've counted four chutes that got out." What he left unsaid was that six didn't get out. I had a sinking feeling we must be next in line for buckling up our parachutes and launching into the air.

The crew never talked about the incident in an attempt to wipe it from our minds. I still have a vivid memory of the thought of going to the back of the plane and bailing out. The recollection leaves me inwardly cringing at how close I came to plunging out over German territory.

Chapter 12.   Leadership

Lt. Holler was not alone in direct violation of standard procedures. Other officers also trespassed in different ways. One of our commanding officers–I'll call him Gabe– paraded his Italian girlfriend around the base dressed in a small man's summer suntan uniform with lieutenant bars on each shoulder. That earned him not only the envy he sought, but also the disrespect of the men.

On days when they scrubbed a mission because of poor weather conditions, mechanical issues, or Headquarters' edicts, Gabe insisted we spend the afternoon hours in close-order drills. This training exercise for ground troops had limited utility for aircrews, resulting in more disdain from all four squadrons' crews.

When Gabe failed to acknowledge my salute, another offense, in my opinion, I felt invisible. We enlisted men looked up to our officers as models for good behavior, and we were highly disappointed when they didn't meet those military standards.

I always kept three leaders as models that I could follow: Captain (later promoted to Major) Grant Caywood, Lt. Charles Schwab, and Lt. Lewis Shackleford.

In the course of driving the Axis forces out of Southern France, the 450th Bomb Group targeted beach defenses in the vicinity of the Sainte Maxime on the Gulf of Saint Tropez. Captain Caywood asked me to be his flight engineer on the only night mission I ever flew. At 0220, I showed up at my aircraft, and we took off for our target at 0730. Surprisingly, we encountered no enemy resistance, making this bomb run qualify as a "milk run."

I flew two additional flights to Southern France with Captain Caywood. Each time we flew, his military comportment proved to be exemplary and gave me the sense that this officer remained on my side. It was my privilege to fly with Captain Caywood, whose later military career earned him the Purple Heart, the Air Medal twice, Distinguished Flying Cross (DFC), and six battle stars.

According to the current 450th Bomb Group historian, James Ciborski, Captain Caywood, a veteran pilot, came to the 720th squadron, replacing two previous pilots. The first, Captain Clark J. Wick, died after a mission in late January 1944. Captain Gordon T. Colley then assumed command. Caywood then replaced Colley, who became the chief executive officer of the 720th Squadron.

After discharge, Major Caywood earned an architect degree, returning to Germany to helped restore some of the buildings bombed in WWII. A true patriot, Caywood attempted to reconcile his war involvement of destroying people and property by rebuilding civilian homes.

Lt. Charles Schwab, another officer I held in high regard, was my primary training officer in the States. I would be sorry to leave him behind. Now ready to fly overseas, I didn't know who the pilot would be. The plan involved taking off from Mitchell Field, Long Island, New York, for our unknown destination. I was ready for anything that the military threw at me. I learned you couldn't choose your parents, let alone your commanding officers.

As I started my climb into the plane, I was overjoyed to be greeted by Lt. Schwab, who leaned over and pulled me in the rest of the way,

"Sgt. Harmon, I'm so relieved that you're trained as an aviation mechanic."

This welcoming greeting demonstrated the qualities of an officer and a gentleman, whose concern for others gained the attention and respect of his crew members.

Throughout the nine days, May 11 to May 20, 1944, we ferried a squadron of B-24s over South America—from Natale, Brazil to French West Africa, and on to Italy. Schwab confirmed my first impression: he showed himself to be a highly-capable pilot, easy to work with anytime.

As I recall, Lt. Schwab had served as a replacement pilot for my 720th squadron. Soon after we arrived in Italy, Headquarters assigned Lt. Schwab to the 721st Squadron. Here he distinguished himself as an outstanding combat pilot, earning the Distinguished Flying Cross (DFC) for meritorious action for bringing his ship through "adverse weather conditions, over rugged terrain and surmounting many other major obstacles." The Air Force accolade added: the accomplishment showed "conspicuous and extraordinary achievements." In addition to the DFC, Lt. Schwab earned five bronze stars, six air medals, ATO ribbon, Victory ribbon, and one overseas service bar. All of the enlisted men who had flown with him spoke highly of this pilot.

I flew 15 combat missions with Lt. Lewis Shackleford, including twice to Ploesti, the most highly fortified armament in World War II. Eight years older than me, this exceptional officer had much greater maturity than most other pilots. A pleasant fellow from Georgia, Shackleford demonstrated great calm and confidence throughout the most dangerous missions. Despite some of the worst flak barrage I ever encountered, Lt. Shackleford never wavered from the bomb run. The crew could all depend on this kind of courage. Shackleford and three other crew members survived a parachute jump into Romania and spent long months in a POW camp in Bucharest. For bravery in battle, Lt. Shackleford was awarded the Distinguished Flying Cross.

Memories of these military leaders have served to guide and inspire my behavior. Because I was only 20 years old during these missions, it was only later, after discharge, that I could reflect on how these remarkable military leaders spurred me on to achieve many accomplishments, as well as helped shape my character.

Fig 2. Burl, age 19, college freshman. Prior to induction.

Fig 3. Burl, at 20 years old, with a B-24 Liberator. My position was technical sergeant flight engineer.

Fig 4. B-24, Liberator Bomber, aerial view. The
bomber was used by both Americans and British
who flew missions over Germany and Europe, it was
also known as the Workhorse Bomber.

Fig 5. P-38, pursuit ship.

Fig 6. P-51 with a red rudder (Red Tail)

Fig 7. Tuskegee Airmen. Pilots of the 332nd Fighter Group

Fig 8. 332nd Flight Squadron Tuskegee Airmen taking off in Red Tail P-51s to escort a bombing raid.

Fig 9. B-24s Bombing Concordia Vega oil refinery in Ploesti, Romania in May 1944.

Fig 10. Title of Burl's airplane.

Fig 11. Massive manufacturing of the Consolidated B-24 Liberator bomber near Ft Worth, Texas.

**Fig 12. I took this photo of The Trepaldi family,
Manduria, Italy.**

Fig 13. The Trepaldi sisters from left to right:
Tina age 17, Lavina age 19.

Fig 14. Here I am with Tina and baby Trepaldi.

Fig 15. 720th squadron in flight
photo taken from our right-wing window.

Fig 16. Hanging out with my friend Mike Friebolin (left).

**Fig 17. My war insignias and metals, including the US 15th Airforce ribbon. I was part of the 450th Bomb group,
720th Squadron.**

Fig 18. Major Grant C. Caywood, pilot.

Fig 19. Lt. Charles L. Schwab Jr., pilot.

Fig 20. Lt. Lewis F. Shackleford, pilot.

Chapter 13.   Limping Home

Growing up in Boone, Iowa, population 13,000, the county seat in rural Boone County, I had minimal contact with ethnic groups, such as Italians, Greeks, and Jews. The dominant nationalities were Swedish, Norwegian, Danish, and German, except the Canakes family, who were Greek, and owned a clothing store. With such narrow horizons, I admit to having my share of stereotypes, mainly of Jewish people. Of course, I believed that Jews were small people, in other words, short of stature, had large noses, and typically kept to themselves. Greeks were pretty much the same.

And then I met First Lieutenant Harold E. Fine, our navigator and official censor, who told the crew he was Jewish. He was, in fact, a fun-loving, out-going, handsome, over-six-feet-tall fellow, who loved puffing on his cigars. For a navigator, the crew found him to be an easy-going guy. It wasn't only Harry that caused me to reverse my thinking. I had a huge eye-opener as I met guys from various ethnic backgrounds: Portuguese, Hawaiian, English, Russian, Irish, Polish, and others of ethnically mixed origins. As I recall, I never personally encountered Black service members on our airbase.

The Air Corps was different in one significant respect, rank was not a factor. Once we were on a plane, it was first names only. Camaraderie and genuine friendship were a natural result of this lack of hierarchy. Such bonding was based on our common interdependence.

On one notable long-distance mission, for which we received double credit, our lives changed drastically. The bomb run went well, and as we turned off the target, a burst of flak took out our #3 engine. Simultaneously, Harry screamed over the intercom: "God damn it! I've been hit!"

I scrambled down from the top turret and, along with Vic the bombardier, was shocked to see Harry holding his right leg, turning a deadly white, ready to faint. Flak cut a deep gash in his right thigh. Vic and I hurried to help Harry. Tearing open the first aid kit, we stared at the contents.

"What the hell?" Vic yelled, "This is all we have: a small pouch of sulfa powder, a stash of gauze bandage, and a tiny roll of adhesive tape."

We scattered sulfa powder on Harry's wound, wrapped his leg with gauze, and secured it with the adhesive tape. I gave him water from my canteen and eased him into a sitting position to keep him alert. I will never forget the measure of his bravery. Instead of leaning back, Harry spread out a map of the area over his lap. His face remained as white as cotton, while he studied how to manage our situation best, as our plane had lost engine three and dropped out of formation. A lone duck is a sitting duck for enemy fighter planes.

The pilot, Jack Holler, yelled, "How's Harry doing? Ask him if we should try to land in Switzerland."

Harry's wound was bound but still bleeding, and he was going into shock.

"It's about the same distance, three hours. Let's head home." Harry responded.

We'd been told a landing in Switzerland, although a neutral country, would mean we would still be held in custody, and the Army required us to make every effort to escape, or we'd be court-martialed.

About that time, someone yelled, "Harmon, get back up in the turret and start firing into the sun."

No sooner had I returned to my .50-caliber, than I looked over my left shoulder and saw two Focke-Wulf 190s with their big black crosses on the wings directly headed our way. I fired a few rounds into the sun—that's where fighters target you. As it turned out, we were fortunate; the planes turned east and disappeared.

About an hour later, I was able to breathe a sigh of relief as we finally crossed the East Coast of Italy. Hallelujah! We knew we were nearly home. I could daydream about a landing in Switzerland with the prospect of meeting pretty girls at the University of Bern. But the Italian Coast provided the safety to daydream. To this day, I can still remember how menacing those Focke-Wulfs looked. Scared out of my mind is an understatement. Our plane limped home on three engines. I was unspeakably grateful that we had escaped the enemy fighters. An ambulance met the plane and picked Harry up for the hospital, while I reported the incidents to the ground crew chief about the failed engine and Harry's wounds.

"Listen," Mike had told everybody when I was late, "You fuckers, don't touch a thing on Ro's bunk. He'll be back.

He's just running behind." It was standard practice for us to designate who got the personal items we'd left behind, if we failed to come back. (When the young woman in Cuba pointed to me and called me Rojo, a nickname was created. The shortened version, Ro, was adopted by my friends.)

More than a half-hour late for our scheduled return, and running later than the rest of the crew, I trekked the two blocks to our barracks carrying my heavy flight bags. "Hi Mike, we've had one hell of an ordeal. Glad we made it back."

I remember very clearly that Mike hugged me, a joyful end to a near disaster. I knew then he was the brother I never had. I pulled out my guitar, and we sang some "Golden Oldies" that comforted both of us.

My steadfast reflection after this harrowing trip: I went into the service as a boy, and I was coming back as a man.

Chapter 14. A Three-Day Pass to Rome: A Close Call

Halfway through a tour of duty in Italy, the military allotted each air crew member a three-day pass to Rome. Such "liberty," as it was called, is expected in the military, but this one was memorable.

At the end of twenty-five missions, our crew of 10 guys mounted aboard the G.I. truck and hauled around to view several points of interest in the ancient city: the Coliseum, Vatican City, the Appian Way, and the Catacombs, among others. I turned down a welcome greeting from Pope Pius XII from sheer stupidity, probably related to my Baptist resistance to Catholicism (funny, my second wife is a practicing Catholic). Afterwards, I heard how gracious the Pope was, and knew I would have enjoyed meeting him.

Instead, I wandered around with Melvin Deem, one of my waist-gunner buddies, awestruck by the sheer number of antiquities. I found the oversized statuary to be particularly appealing, especially the towering statues of David and St. Peter. Up close and personal, I discovered that St. Peter's right large toe had been worn slick by the fervent kisses of believers. Who would have thought such devotion possible?

As we moved into the Catacombs, we felt a hush as we witnessed the bones of faithful Christians piled high on both sides of the cave. The skulls seemed to leer at us, two displaced boys from another land. The site also displayed chunks of wood, purported to be from the original cross of the Crucifixion. I kept my doubts to myself, because I knew wood could never endure all those centuries as intact as these artifacts appeared.

After our tour, Melvin and I hired a Roman resident, Antonio, whose passable English made it possible for him to hire out as a guide. We knew Antonio felt pleased he could be of service to Americans, using his knowledge of the English language to show off his beautiful ancient city. We romped through his walking tour, which led us to the Coliseum. Antonio pointed out the expansiveness of the structure, the size of two football fields, and despite centuries of neglect and a major war, incredibly complete.

Antonio directed us to the former ground-floor prisons located at one end of the building, where Christians were systematically persecuted and tortured. It was chilling to think of the martyrs led to their death, torn to pieces by starved wild animals. I shuddered at the grossness of these killings.

"Soldier, you fuck my sister—two dollars," a small boy rushed up to us and shouted. Although I was only 20-years old, I knew this was not right. My own sister at home was just 13, and these boys were selling sisters that age or even younger. Of course, neither Melvin nor I had any interest in this tawdry trade. When we gave the boy some lira coins, he murmured "molto grazie," and moved on. "War is hell," I thought, when I recognized the length to which hungry people will go for survival.

Once back in the truck, the pilot in charge of the "tourist trip," announced,

"Listen, guys, we've got another day here."

"I'll be a son-of-a-bitch, Melvin. The army's getting softhearted. They've given us another day on leave. Wonder what's going on?"

Back at the base, I found our veteran crew had initially been assigned to this newly arrived B-24, Model H., a kind of reward for our efforts—and our survival. But there was a shift in plans when the operations officer reassigned that plane to the new crew just coming into Manduria, our air base in Italy. I felt a twinge of irritation about having had to forfeit that mission, but at the same time, a rush of elation for having had another day to keep exploring Rome with Antonio and Melvin.

The next day, I learned what happened to that new crew when returning crews gave us the horrendous news. "Our" recently delivered B-24 went down in flames from a direct hit from anti-aircraft fire. Flak blew off the right wing, and nobody got out. Every man lost in a single moment.

My crew and I were supposed to be on that plane, I kept saying to myself. If not for the extra day in Rome, we would have been on that combat flight, and met the fate of those who will never return. I exploded in tears and stumbled over to my bunk. The shocking experience stayed with me for months, and haunts me today, 78 years later.

Reflecting upon this, I knew then that God had a purpose for my life after the war. To this day, I still feel overwhelmed when I realize I could have been on that fallen aircraft. As an institution, the military would never have mourned the loss of our crew. I felt woefully resigned to the Army's viewpoint.

"You're expendable, but the plane is not." The tragedy, of course, is that both men and plane were gone forever.

Chapter 15.   Combat Missions Completed

Some dates are memorable. October 7, 1945, holds a special place in my life. That's the date I finished my final 38th mission, but earning credit for 51, since some of the more dangerous missions were given double credit. Now, for a furlough home, and then another round with the military after I'm declassified and reassigned.

Goodbyes to my 720th-crew squadron were serious, even solemn, events, mainly because friendships fashioned in life-threatening times were now relegated to the immediate past. In all likelihood, we would never see one another again.

A deep sense of sorrow settled over my second parting, this time with the Trepaldi family, having mutually adopted one another. Papa Trepaldi (all 5'2" of him) and I embraced, and he kissed me on both cheeks. I left them weeping, knowing I'd never see this beautiful Italian family of ten again. No kissing or hugging of those charming girls, of course, but I took away the image of their waving me goodbye.

Farewells could be promising occasions, as well. My radio operator, and wonderful friend and brother, Mike Friebolin, still had a few missions left to fly, while I had completed mine. Although we intended to meet again in the states—so full of goodbye promises—the years wore on, and much to my deep regret, we never reunited. Apparently, our lives were both entirely too involved readapting to civilian life to take the time to find one another.

After completing combat missions in October 1944, I was ready to leave. I finally packed up, gave my guitar to a grateful picker, and flew from Manduria to Naples for eventual passage home on a troop ship. I didn't realize that we were seriously overloaded on that B-24 with thirteen guys and their baggage in the bomb bay.

Naples was socked in with a turbulent weather front, and coming in for the landing with our heavy load, we hit a down draft and plummeted 1200 feet. I was at least as frightened by this incident as flying through flak on a bomb run. How ironic it would be to go down after flying all those missions! We made it okay, but all of us silently departing from that plane were too terrified to speak.

One more overnight before boarding the troop ship, and, as always, our assigned makeshift barracks with double-decker G.I. bunks lacked one essential comfort: mattresses. The standard joke—good thing the bunks were made of soft pine. But we didn't care. We were going home.

The lieutenant assigned me to manage the mainly untrained military guards onboard the ship, who were put on duty as spotters for German submarines. It goes without saying that amateur guards searching for periscopes in the darkness of an October night have little to report.

On one pleasant occasion, when I was making rounds to check on each guard station, I heard a voice calling: "Guard! Guard!"

I raced over, expecting the worst: a submarine ready to attack! "What's the matter?"

"Nothing," said a seaman baker from the "galley" (the navy term for kitchen). "I just wanted to give the guard a steak sandwich. But since he's not here, you take it and I'll get him another one."

After years of bland army food without flavor, the tenderloin sandwich, my first taste of heaven, had to be the finest one I'd ever eaten.

The voyage back was not without concerns. Our troopship was a Matson Line Summer Cruiser with diesel engines, not intended to ply the North Atlantic during a winter storm. The ship, built around a huge timber some 90 to 100 feet long, pitched in the rough seas, creating eerie cracking sounds that could be heard throughout the ship. Totally freaked out by the sound of destiny, I asked a veteran navy chief petty officer if the ship was likely to break apart.

"Nope, not yet anyway," he said, and shrugged, indifferent to my misery.

Receiving no comfort from this guy, I also faced the prospect of seasickness. Men, far more macho than I, were heaving over the deck rails, and my turn to feel nauseous came the fourth day out. Laying low, sucking on oranges, I managed to keep my stomach contents intact.

Yearning to see the Statue of Liberty in the New York Harbor, I was cruelly disappointed when we landed in

Boston. But at least we were on sacred American ground again, so I quickly gave up my griping to being grateful.

During the voyage, I had gotten acquainted with Sean, another G.I. from Boston. When Sean learned that I planned to go to a hotel, he insisted,

"Oh no you won't. I'll take you home to my family, they'll love you."

My fond memory of Bostonians always brings up that delightful Irish family as well as another friendly incident. The next day, I walked from Sean's house to the station to catch the next bus to Des Moines, Iowa, and was having a tough time managing the two oversized barracks bags. A young guy, 15 or 16, raced by me, and hearing me winded with effort, turned around and came back. "Can I carry your bags, soldier?" What a warm welcome home from the hazards of war. This is the last genuine welcome I received on that disappointing furlough home.

Chapter 16. The Fizzled Furlough

Pulling into the Des Moines, Iowa bus station, I eagerly jumped down from the bus steps, and rushed to the nearby YMCA. Tomorrow morning, I planned to catch the early train to Boone, my hometown. Home. What a beautiful sound. "No place like home..." I hummed, as my homecoming dream included a joyous welcoming from my folks and sister Pansy, meeting up this evening with the high school girl of my dreams, Carolyn, now at Stevens College, and seeing old buddies and their families.

On the way home, I stopped over at Columbia, Missouri, to visit Carolyn at college. Once I located her dormitory, I called from the desk, "Hi Carolyn, I'm home for my furlough after nearly three years away. I'd love to see you if you're available."

"Hi Burl, it's good to hear your voice. I've had a terrible case of the flu and will have to stay in tonight. But let's plan to go to church tomorrow. I should be feeling better."

A crushing disappointment, but still hopeful, I put on my uniform that morning, hoping I could convince her to get together after the war. Church over, Carolyn indicated she still wasn't feeling very good and wanted to get back to her room. I stammered, "goodbye," "great seeing you," and somehow got back on the bus to Des Moines.

Homecoming turned out to be weird. Dad had only recently returned from Detroit and wasn't paying attention to the family. Wanting to do his patriotic duty, he had worked there the last six months in a war defense factory. Now, he had to turn his attention to the automobile body and fender shop he left. He and Mom weren't really talking to one another, and sister Pansy had her own friends, and was preoccupied elsewhere. As I recall, we didn't even have a Christmas tree or decorations. Since I had to leave three days before the holiday, I missed both Christmas and New Year's Eve. Worse, I never saw any of my high school buddies, who were still in the service or prisoners of war. Everything seemed disheartening for me. One more adventure awaited me, though.

Much to my amazement and frustration, Mom had put one of my letters I had written home from Italy into the Des Moines Register, detailing my random thoughts: what a good son I was; I'm never in trouble, unlike some guys; and even married men were having sex with the local Italian girls. I also let her know I would be seriously looking for a girlfriend when I got home. A local farm girl, Telva Bibler, who worked at the newspaper, wrote me back, inviting me to meet her in Des Moines. She was quite insistent about pursuing me: "I want to be your girlfriend."

Oh dear, meeting Telva for the first time, I discovered that, although quite pleasant, she wasn't exactly what I had in mind for a girlfriend. Having lost two front teeth, she covered a bleak smile with a furtive hand over her mouth. I felt sorry for her. When I met her father, he acted the bully part, and put other guys down to build himself and his sons up. The prospect of going further with this romance had little appeal. Still, I visited her that sad furlough period, meeting Mr. Bibler and his two sons, both of whom had been exempted from the draft. One afternoon, while chatting with Telva, her sister, and her mother in the kitchen, I noticed the guys heading outdoors to finish the chores. As he marched out the back door, Bibler turned and shouted,

"Well, Harmon, I see you like to hang out with the womenfolk, instead of rolling up your sleeves like us men." Taken aback by his remark since he hadn't even asked me to join him, it never occurred to me that was his backhanded invitation for me to join "the men."

Mr. Bibler's solution to my post-war job problem was even less inviting. He recommended I take out a $20,000 loan, buy a tractor, lease a quarter section of his land, and raise corn. The implicit message: marry his daughter and live happily ever after.

Having never had a girlfriend, I wasn't sure what to do, and I took the wrong road. To assuage her parents about my intentions, I bought her a ring and proceeded to actively engage in as much smooching as possible. We spent the following year writing letters back and forth, but I knew I couldn't keep up the pretense.

As I reflected on that end-of-combat furlough in 1944, I was stunned at limiting myself to Telva, whose conversation was dull, disjointed, and hardly up to my college friends, Carolyn and others. And with all the disappointments of the past month and dashed dreams, I couldn't get out of Boone fast enough.

Like consuming too many fizzled Coca-Colas® when I was training in Texas, the fizzled furlough put a stop to my dreaming, and energized me to focus on my upcoming military assignment.

Chapter 17.   Mustering Out

Although I left disgruntled with the furlough, my enthusiasm picked up after returning to the base. It was time for a new post.

Reclassification after combat duty involved a series of tests in assessing skills and interests. Mine turned out to be clerical-verbal acuity rather than mechanical. Some of the questions were no-brainers, but I'm still not sure what the Minnesota Multiphasic had in mind with this one:

"Which would you rather do: change the spark plugs of a '39 chevy or have a picnic lunch with a girlfriend?" I didn't know how to change the spark plugs of any vehicle!

The teaching assignment at Mountain Home, Idaho airbase, 60 miles east of Boise, was the most rewarding experience of my military tenure. My job consisted of acquainting the officers—pilot, copilot, navigator, and bombardier—and crew with a review of the function of each battle station on the B-24: nose, tail, ball turret, top turret, and two wing windows, each equipped with twin .50 caliber machine guns.

Training new crews marked a turning point in my life. I learned that imparting knowledge and sharing my experiences gave me considerable confidence and high satisfaction. I relished being in charge of the group—both officers and enlisted men.

Another benefit: who could have predicted that I would be assigned to the only classroom on the base that was air-conditioned? This job offered a far cry from doing maintenance on the B-24 flight line, the assignment for those who tested high on the mechanical option.

I must have impressed the young lieutenant, who headed my department, and who offered me an unexpected compliment: carving out the direction my civilian life would take, including college degrees and a teaching and administrative career.

"Harmon, you're going to be a pillar of your community someday."

During my stint as an instructor, Franklin Roosevelt died, the German nation capitulated because the Nazi regime disintegrated, and the European war ended. Citizens eager to return to their normal lives celebrated Victory in Europe (V-E Day).

Attention then turned to the war in the Pacific. The U.S. dropped the first atomic bomb on Hiroshima, Japan, obliterating the city and killing 70,000 and 135,000 of its residents. Yet, the military refused to surrender. A second bomb, three days later on Nagasaki, even more powerful, turned humans into shadows on the sidewalk, bringing Japan to its knees. The Emperor conceded. Hostilities ended; the world achieved a semblance of peace. The big question now: how do we pick up the pieces?

I didn't give much thought to this overwhelming question. Instead, I focused entirely on mustering out of the military and leaving it forever behind. Nothing much mattered to me then. When I finally reached my hometown on October 15, 1945, I made a personal style decision. I would never wear olive drab again, or brown for that matter, after nearly three years wearing monotonous military garb.

After jumping off the bus, I headed for the Holst Hotel Coffee Shop, still my favorite, and ordered a chicken-fried steak with gravy and mashed potatoes. For dessert, apple pie with vanilla ice cream—definitely not Army chow!

Feeling expansive, I stashed my bags at the coffee shop and decided to shop for civilian clothes. I had 1500 dollars waiting for me in the bank that I was itching to spend. Nothing but the best, top-of-the-line quality and high prices.

But old clothing habits die hard. When I entered Ennen's Clothing Store after jumping off the bus, I felt drawn to the dark brown gabardine trousers on the model. Brown trousers required the rest of the outfit blend, so I pulled out the perfect brown houndstooth jacket from the rack, then moving over to the shoe department, I picked out matching brown Florsheim shoes at the monstrous price of $10. The table display showed a splendid Oxford shirt, twice the price of broadcloth, and I added it to the pile.

I paid the bill, barely looking at the price. I was on top of the world. Sauntering out in my new, sartorial fashion, I began wandering around the hometown, familiarizing myself with specialty shops and hangouts of my youth. Within a half-hour, I heard a beloved voice, my father's. We hugged, and finally, I was home and safe, but only for a few moments.

In a jumble of words, Dad told me he was divorced from my mother and living in an apartment. He mumbled that Mom had her own apartment with Pansy, now 14 years old. Seldom have I had such a jolt! I staggered, and feeling faint, I bent over with fear. What will happen to me? They had sold our home. I had no place to go. I had a sense of terror about how everything could change so fast.

I stayed in my father's apartment for a few nights. What haunted me was concern over my mother and sister. How could I help them? And then the girlfriend, Telva. After much personal agony, I severed the relationship and decided to move on.

"What do I do with the ring?" she wept.

"You can throw it in the Des Moines River for all I care."

End of story. I felt truly sorry for Telva.

I later learned that Telva was devastated at the breakup, lost a considerable amount of weight, and her family was deeply concerned about her health.

Job! I needed to do something to occupy my mind after that episode. I applied at the Rexall store, but they didn't have an opening, and I reluctantly crossed the street to the cut-rate drug store, where they hired me on the spot. Doing something worthwhile seemed to settle my emotional turmoil. Another jolt! Within a few days, the girl I held in romantic fantasy, Carolyn, had become engaged. This news was too brutal to accept.

First, my parents' breakup, then stumbling out of a relationship with Telva, and now losing any chance with Carolyn; it all had me spinning.

Mom and Pansy soon moved out to Grandma's farm to be caregivers for Grandma Christian. I experienced a wave of relief. I could focus on getting my own act together. Later, Mom registered for college classes, completing a secondary education degree, although she supported herself and Pansy with non-teaching jobs.

Dad moved into another apartment he planned to later share with Fernie, his new girlfriend and his soon-to-be wife. That left his apartment—the upstairs rooms of a Methodist minister's widow—available for rent. The widow and I got along famously. I was saddened when Dad married Fernie that December of 1945. Still, I recognized it was a good choice for him after years of being unhappy with my mother.

God gave me the courage to be open to new possibilities when I came across the junior college Dean, John Thorngren. We arranged for a conversation in his office, a fateful meeting that turned my life around. Through his persuasion, I finished enough hours to earn an AA degree, and move on to complete my baccalaureate My church sent me to a summer retreat where I met others like me, seeking a purpose and career in life. These post-discharge events are how I became a high school teacher and administrator, spending 40 fruitful years in the profession. At age 97, blessed with two guitar students, I continue my love of passing on knowledge.

Chapter 18.   Memorable Characters

As I reflect on the memorable characters I met during military service, I found that those who worked for team enhancement were my special folks. Being an aircrew member taught me the value and necessity of being a team player. Almost all of the guys I worked with had the team qualities needed to carry out our missions successfully: cooperation, communication, solidarity, fellowship, and joint effort. The bomb group is a typical example of teamwork. Each crew member carries out his specific job while also tuned into the other crew members' situations, such as when I was injured while on a training mission and had immediate care from three crew members.

I should begin with the most memorable of all characters, Lt. Harold D. Fine, my intrepid navigator. "Just call me Harry," he said. I remember him as the most egalitarian officer on the base.

Some crew members were memorable because they were great team players. Lt. John Fredd, my copilot, a few years older than me, was tall, good-looking, and a ready conversationalist. We shared guard duty one night to protect our plane from espionage, a constant threat. The enemy's favorite trick involved inserting a bomb in the tread of the landing gear tire. On landing or take off, the tire would blow up, causing the aircraft to crash.

We often exchanged numerous ideas about life, initiated by John, who carefully followed the news. With time on our hands during guard duty one night, we started talking about our future. I had never considered the possibility of the war being over, much less what I would do after military service.

John, on the other hand, had given it a lot of thought.

"I read in *Yank* magazine that President Roosevelt signed a bill providing free college to any veteran. Do you think you'd take advantage of that?"

I had finished my third semester at Boone Junior College before being drafted, but never had a clue I could earn a college degree. His words gave me hope.

"Yeah, I'll check it out. I might try my hand at being an English teacher."

A few days later, my friend, promoted to pilot with a new crew, suffered the loss of his life, his plane, and his crew, annihilated by enemy anti-aircraft fire. I felt paralyzed with grief that I'd never see him again, because in John's death the world had lost a precious treasure.

Another favorite crew member, "Pappy Cole," was our "old guy," a former machinist in civilian life, but a waist gunner in the Air Corps. We all wondered why a much older, already balding guy had this kind of dangerous assignment when he was a master machinist. His easy-going personality and good humor saved the day on many occasions.

"Pappy, how come you're a waist gunner? You're too old to be an aerial gunner."

Pappy replied, "The reason I'm here is that the draft board called up my number only a few days before I would have been 37 and exempt from military service."

"Pappy," I said, "I don't know why you're here, but you can fly waist gunner for me anytime."

Another crew member piped up, "That's a shame, Pappy. They lost a good machinist when they drafted you."

We all had a particular measure of respect for Pappy, who never felt sorry for himself, despite his misaligned Air Corps job.

Lt. "Jarm" Jarmolovich, a sharp clean-cut kid, a year younger than I, hailed from Hartford, Connecticut, one of those early tree huggers. He had one of those unpronounceable last names that we kidded him about.

Jarm had a sense of humor, second to none. While cruising over the Atlantic from Natal, Brazil to Dakar, French West Africa, he had a brilliant idea.

"Let's hook up your guitar to the throat mic, so the Nazis in the submarine down there will be confused." I wonder if the U-boat sailor didn't say to his buddy, "Was machen diese verrückten Amerikaner bis jetzt?" ("What are those crazy Americans up to now?") Our pilot only shook his head in bewilderment.

My heart goes out to Jarm, shot down over Vienna and held in prison camps in Hungary, Germany, and Austria while serving on another crew. Jarm survived that experience and flourished in his hometown of Hartford with his wife of 65 years and a family of six children. He died in 2015.

Many of the crew members that I felt drawn to were ordinary guys like me, but they played an essential role on the team. Jon Leahy, one of my waist gunners, grew up in Leon, Iowa, a nice quiet farm boy. The two of us had filled out the quota for the Aviation Mechanic School, and we trained together before moving into the 720th Squadron. Always calm and competent, Jon handled his weapon with skill and accuracy.

Mac, a fellow gunner, saved up his liquor supplied by the Air Corps and often came to my bunk after a mission or on one of our non-flying days.

"Are you flying tomorrow, Ro?" If I said "no," he'd walk over to his bunk, pull out his booze, return to my bunk, and say,

"Let's have a party. You play the old favorites, and I'll drink." and asked me to play the guitar. I had a sense my guitar playing to these lonely guys helped build team spirit.

Some men were more than crew members. In addition to Melvin Deem, who shared my furlough in Rome, I had two other very close friends, Al Chartier and Mike Friebolin. Like brothers, we hung out together, looked out for each other, and had a special connection.

Let me start with Al Chartier, a ball turret gunner, about my height (5'7"), who passed for an Italian with his dark skin. Because Al had a smattering of Italian, he was the one who discovered the Trepaldi family, who laundered our uniforms weekly. My main goal was to catch a glimpse, and maybe more, of the two older Trepaldi girls. Al swore up and down that Tina had asked him to "caress" her, but that story is improbable, as the girls were never left alone without one or another parent. At the time, I felt so envious, but I lacked the nerve to make any similar overtures to the other sister, Lavina.

I always knew Al to be a high-risk taker and discovered he had been in a combat accident while on a mission before his discharge. Sadly, shortly after his discharge, I learned Al had crashed into a concrete abutment and was killed instantly. Is it possible that the military plane accident had left him with untreated PTSD, a condition that could have precipitated erratic behavior?

I had another friend during my training missions, Mike Friebolin, my radio operator. Mike and I both went through all the B-24 training sessions, and I liked to think of him as my brother-in-arms. In contrast, we were a picture. Mike hailed from Chicago, probably didn't finish high school, ran around with the fast crowd, and had a strong urge to drink whatever alcoholic beverage came his way. You could sum up Mike's life with this phrase: booze, broads, and bandying around. Mike was the kind of guy who never took matters too seriously, a hang-loose character with no plans.

My life in the much slower lane of small-town living, which was school and church focused, had shaped me into a rule-abider, steady, with a no-risk approach to living. My new goal after discharge—get my college degree.

Despite the differences, Mike and I were on the same wavelength. Mike loved acting the role of big brother and was only too free with advice. When I started smoking in May 1944, because I thought I was missing out on something, Mike raged,

"You dumb bastard, don't you know those things will kill you?" This remark from a guy who smoked like a chimney!

In a candid moment, he turned to me and said quietly,

"My mother would have loved for me to be like you, non-smoking, non-drinking, and not hanging out in bad company." I grinned, then remarked,

"You know, Mike, mothers always want their sons to be a certain way. My mother wants me to be a Baptist preacher, the furthest thing from my mind."

Mike set me straight about brotherhood, a person you could share your thoughts and ideas without fear of reaction. Mike served as the brother I never had. My only experience with brothers was my two uncles, Howard and Bert, who never really liked one another, rarely giving each other any support in all the years I knew them. Although Mike and I were close during our training and combat months, we never connected after the war, a loss I feel today.

The war taught me some valuable lessons, the greatest of which was working with the many diverse personalities and backgrounds I encountered.

Chapter 19.   The Return

One of the most exhilarating rewards of a marriage late in life has been traveling to "faraway places with strange sounding names." Being a son of the Depression with a Mount Everest size poverty script, intermittent traveling had never been on my bucket list.

However, one remarkable trip is rooted in my memory. At 85, I was ready for new challenges. Global Volunteers, an organization focused on placing American teachers overseas, posted an invitation that piqued my curiosity. This company was seeking volunteers to teach American English to residents of a small Italian village in the boot of Italy, Ostuni, eight kilometers from the Adriatic Sea. When I showed the invitation to my wife, Nanette, she was elated, and we decided to leave as soon as they could schedule us.

The program offered to board us for two weeks for an individual fee of approximately the price of a cruise. Since I had a yen to revisit Rome's ancient, fabled city, we found the invitation compelling. Furthermore, the location had remarkable proximity to a significant period in my life, located only a few miles from the US Army Air Corps WWII base in Manduria, Italy.

Nanette and I flew to Rome, spent a week acting like typical tourists, hanging out at the Vatican, various museums, and the Colosseum. When we landed in Ostuni, our destination for two weeks, we encountered an ancient city, known as "The White Town," for its dazzling white walls and white painted architecture. As a tourist mecca, it attracted a heavy influx of foreign residents, especially in the warmer months. A smaller city of 32,000 in winter, the population swells to 100,000 in summer. We were entranced with the tiered medieval city layout with its ancient churches, restaurants hidden in caves, and exquisite gift shops.

On our first day of volunteering, we taught English to seniors in the town's Senior Club and worked with foster children in a care center. Senior teaching offered both of us enchanting experiences. Nanette used colored photos from recipe books brought from home to teach English words for food and cooking. Once I found out that my students could not pronounce a single English word, I used my familiar guitar to train them in melody and rhythm. The old favorites, "Take Me Out to The Ballgame," "Swing Low Sweet Chariot," "When the Saints Go Marching In," and other rousing songs could be heard throughout the entire building.

Teaching English to recalcitrant middle-school boys turned out to be our least successful effort. The boys, failing at home and school, were unmotivated. Most appeared irritable, too restless to sit for any period of time. One youngster, about 12 years old, had been waiting for days for his dad to pick him up and try one more time to integrate him into the home setting. The father never picked the boy up, and we realized he had been cast out because of his behavior problems. We did not see a happy ending for this child.

As we neared the end of our first week of volunteering, we engaged an English-speaking local to guide us in his old Mercedes to nearby towns and places of interest.

At the time, I had no idea he planned to drive us to Manduria, 50 miles from Ostuni, where I had been stationed from May to October in 1944. At that time, I regarded Manduria as a tiny village with dirt roads. Now we discovered it to be a thriving, modern, small town with one of the squares (piazza) featuring a bronze statue of an American soldier, decorated as a hero and liberator.

Walking around the town's perimeter, we had another discovery—an archeological park from ancient Manduria with remains of military defenses revealed that Roman troops had occupied the area.

We encountered a double line of walls comprised of rectangular stone blocks put together without mortar and a broad ditch in front. Next to this structure, an ancient cemetery had multiple gravesites, their size compatible with the occupants' status. We stared at the open graves, evenly cut out of the ground, an entire column of graves lined up and down in evenly spaced units. We were the only observers there, and for a moment, we felt a bit like amateur archeologists discovering this ancient treasure.

Much to my dismay, I came to realize that the Italian family I had come to know and love in 1944 were no longer living in Manduria. The Trepaldi family, typical of the town's poverty-stricken residents, were abandoned when German troops fled, taking their crops, live animals, and other subsistence. Although we arrived months after the German rout, the town had not recovered from their losses. I can still feel the pain in my heart for the little I could do for them. But I am so grateful that I could show Nanette where I grew from boy to man.

Our final evening before leaving, the senior center treated us to round after round of homemade Italian pizza. Nanette's choice, the artichoke and tomato with rich cheese topped over crispy crust, "absolutely delicious," she claimed. My choice, any piece I could get my hands on. Those war survivors, who were now adept at singing American songs, treated us to their medley of favorites and under my tutelage, not a syllable mispronounced.

Holding close to memories, both of my combat experiences out of Manduria, and the renewed opportunity to connect with Italian survivors, I felt a twinge of sadness as I boarded the plane to return home.

Bibliography and Photo Credits

Front cover: Top: "The Sandman a B-24 Liberator, piloted by Robert Sternfels," Wikimedia, 2004.
  Bottom: 450th Bomb Group Memorial Association website, www.450thbg.com

Back cover: Top: "B-24s Bombing Concordia Vega Oil Refinery," Wikipedia,
  Bottom: 450th Bomb Group Memorial Association website, www.450thbg.com

450th Bomb Group Memorial Association website for Figures 1, 3, 15, 18, 19, 20, www.450thbg.com

Cover Photo of Burl Harmon: Flight training graduation photo.

Photos in the Public Domain:
  Wikimedia: Figures 4, 5, 6, 7, 8, 9, 11.

Photos from the personal archives of Burl Harmon: Figures 2, 10, 12, 13, 14, 16, 17.

Cowart, Clarence P. *A Fallen Eagle: A WWII B-24 Pilot in the 15th Air Force with the 450th BG "Cottontails."* Dog Ear Publishing, 2009, pp. 114-115.

Fulton, Mandie, et al. "Cottontails." Official Publication of the 450th Bombardment Group (H) Memorial Association, Volume 23, No. 1 and 2, 2021.

Personal Communication with Jim Ciborski, Historian, 450th Bomb Group, April-June 2021. Jim Ciborski is the son of James R. Ciborski, a fellow airman who served with me in the 720th squadron.

Raiford, Neil Hunter. *Shadow: A Cottontail Bomber Crew in World War II.* McFarland, 2004.

Worthington, Mark. *Official Home of the 450th Bomb Group Memorial Association*, 450th Bomb Group

Memorial Association, 1999,
www.450thbg.com/real/index.shtml.

About The Author

Harmon's stories kept accumulating about his WWII experiences, and the COVID-19 pandemic offered a perfect opportunity to write them up. The author retired from the Kansas City School System after nearly 40 years of teaching and administration. He lives with his wife in Bellingham, WA, and has traveled widely in Europe, South America and Mexico. Harmon's guitar picking brings music into the lives of family, friends, and seniors in care centers.